REVIEWS

"Pastor Elsie Otegbade, in her simple storytelling style, succeeds in turning the biblical Ruth into our regular next-door neighbor in this short tome. Ruth is the riveting and uncommon story of a young woman who, after being widowed, made an unusual choice to stay with her husband's mother and succeeds through her exceptional mix of character, diligence, and humility to work both of them into Jewish nobility. You will fall for Otegbade's charm in the way she beautifully wove her own life tapestry into a Bible story. It is what makes this book all the more insightful on how God and humanity constantly work to produce unusual outcomes in the life of anyone that chooses to accept Jesus as Lord and Savior."

Obiageli "Oby" Ezekwesili
Former Vice President of the World Bank and Former
Minister of Education for Nigeria

"Reading through this powerful book rekindled my faith in God. It teaches about putting our trust in God even when everything seems to be falling apart all around us; in using the story of Ruth in the Bible, Otegbade drives the theme of agape love and hope across succinctly. "Being able to count your losses and retrace your steps is so vital to your progress and the future," she writes. This book was an absolute delight to read, and I would recommend it to everyone who has ever faced one form of adversity or another. The lessons to take from it are very powerful. I found it an easy and fun book to read. I absolutely enjoyed it. Pastor Elsie Otegbade tackles the subject of hope and love in a very poignant manner; I look forward to reading more books from the author."

Emem Isong Misodi
Award-winning Nollywood Film producer

"Wow, this is an amazing book: so many life lessons and true-life stories written in a simple but highly impactful way. Bringing the story of Ruth into our contemporary day and drawing so many relatable lessons, it was incredible. Once you start reading this book, you can't stop until you are done because it is loaded with so much value. The Reflections after each chapter are just brilliant. This book is a must-have. I am so privileged to review it. Thank you, Pastor Elsie, and God bless you."

Florence Igboayaka,
Bestselling Author

ELSIE OTEGBADE

HE GIVES HOPE IN ADVERSITY

Overcoming Challenges with lessons from the Book of Ruth

Scripture passages in this book are taken from the New King James Version®. Copyright © 1982 by Thomas Nelson. Used by permission. All rights reserved.

ISBN: 978-1-7359973-0-8

Book interior formatted by Anne McLaughlin, Blue Lake Design.

Published by: TRINITYRISE LLC, 400 Del Antico Avenue #400,

Oakley, Ca 94561.

Author's contact:
Website: www.elsieotegbade.com
Email: info@elsieotegbade.com

Printed in the United States of America.

DEDICATION

Firstly, I want to dedicate this book to the Almighty God,
who poured out His grace generously over my life.
I am eternally grateful to Him.

Secondly, to my husband and wonderful children:
Though a blended family, Jesus made the difference in our lives.
Through Him, we overcame obstacles,
and today we all stand victoriously in Him.

Finally, to all those whose life will find new meaning after
reading this book, I want you to know God is not
through with you.

CONTENTS

"The flower that blooms in adversity is the most rare and beautiful of all."

— THE EMPEROR (CHARACTER IN *MULAN*, DIRECTED BY BARRY COOK AND TONY BANCROFT, DISNEY STUDIOS, 1998)

ACKNOWLEDGMENTS

A fter writing and not publishing my first book *Putting on the New Man* over 25 years ago (I lost the manuscript and I did not have it stored anywhere, unfortunately), I just never bothered writing again afterwards.

I want to thank Florence Igboayaka, whose 30-day book writing challenge got me writing again.

My appreciation to members of my current church, Redeemed Christian Church of God (RCCG), Jesus Fort, California, for their continued support and love towards my husband and me. Starting a church in California from ground zero was tough, but you all made it easy.

My sincere appreciation and gratitude to Mrs. Oby Ezekwesili, former Minister of Education of Nigeria, former Vice President of the World Bank and 2018 Nominee for Nobel Peace Prize; to Pastor Deola Mensah, Special

Assistant to the Wife of the General Overseer of the RCCG and a Province Pastor of RCCG; to Emem Isong Misodi, an award-winning Nollywood Film Producer and CEO of Royal Arts Academy, Nigeria; for taking time out of their very busy schedules to read review this book for me.

Finally, special gratitude to my beloved husband, Pastor Femi Otegbade. I could never have made a better choice for myself. Your love, support, and encouragement to do whatever I set my heart to accomplish is second to none. My greatest cheerleader and my hero!

To my children, Lola, Bunmi, Pearl, Diran, Victor, OreOluwa and OpeOluwa, and my grandchildren, Zoe and Zion. I am so proud of the decent, intelligent and God fearing young men and woman you have each become, impacting your generation in your different ways. Thank you for making me proud. You are my world!

FOREWORD

I first met Pastor Elsie Otegbade in the Apapa parish of the RCCG, in the early 1990s. It was easy to become friends with her joyful, cheerful nature. Very faithful and committed in church, and one thing that singled her out was the desire to grow in spiritual matters. So over the years, it has been delightful to watch and see how she has turned out for God. I am also not surprised as to how God is using her to touch lives.

This short book is full of nuggets and very impactful. It is a study of the book of Ruth interspersed with the author's personal experience.

I found it quite engaging and more than a few times stopped to reflect on the faithfulness of our great God to reach and settle the solitary in families, even as He promised in Psalm 68:6.

A few things stand out worthy of note:

Adversity comes to us all in different forms. No matter who you are or how highly placed, you will face low points in life that may shake you to the core. Sometimes we find ourselves in uncomfortable situations, which may be a result of a disastrous decision as in the case of Naomi and her family relocating to Moab. It could also be due to the envy and jealously of others, as in the case of Joseph, who was sold into slavery. It could just also be something you had no control over, as in Ruth. However, God is always merciful and will always make a way when we call upon Him to help.

Adversities may be devastating at the beginning, but whatever the Devil meant for evil, God is able to turn it around for good. Adversities are meant to toughen us and turn our gaze towards God, our only source of help. The author mentioned that in the midst of severe challenges, Ruth clung to this God whom she had learned about from Naomi; to trust and call upon. Her situation looked hopeless, but God was there through it all.

The author states that we should not allow adversity to define us, nor should we pick up a victim mentality. The Bible tells us that if we faint in the day of adversity... our strength is small... (Prov. 24:10). We are to keep our values, stand in faithful hope, and trust God to send help at the right time. Ruth did not allow her circumstance to change her core values of chastity, love, respect, and care for Naomi. We are encouraged to be content with what we have and not allow covetousness or envy to becloud our godly values.

Indeed, we shall reap a just reward if we do not faint. One thing that kept ringing in my heart as I read the book is that we must keep hope alive, whether it's for us or a loved one, and not allow discouragement or despair to weigh us down. Ruth listened to wise counsel from Naomi, and in the end, she did not fail God, nor the trust reposed in her by all who came in contact with her.

We see the end result that God always comes through, Ruth got married to Boaz, and the child from that union became the great-grandfather of David—subsequently putting Ruth in the genealogy of Jesus Christ.

It was not only Ruth that received healing—Naomi also did. Joy was restored; God turned her mourning into dancing and gave her beauty for ashes. There is also healing for all that are wounded and broken-hearted because God is a restorer and will restore all that has been lost due to whatever adversity may befall a man.

I encourage you to read this book again and again. The author's personal testimonies are also an indication of God's goodness and faithfulness. That for those who put their trust in the Lord, hope will be restored, and the joy once lost shall be recovered.

We serve a God that we can trust to come through for us regardless of the circumstances and curves life may throw us.

You cannot just give up now... help is on the way.

Adeola Mensah,
Special Assistant to the wife of the General Overseer
and Province Pastor of the Redeemed Christian
Church of God
September, 2020

INTRODUCTION

The book of Ruth in the Bible is the first book that was named after a woman, indeed one of only two books in the Bible named after women.

The story of Ruth typifies the struggles of many women after the loss of a husband. She starts her life afresh and learns to care for herself afresh. She is forced to face the world with her pains and tears with the help of the Holy Spirit, her Comforter. Strength from God keeps her going each day, not knowing what lays ahead but trusting in the God in whom she has believed that her tomorrow will be all right, hoping against hope that joy will come again! The sun will rise again.

In this book, we want to study the life of Ruth, a Moabitess, who got to know God. But instead of life becoming better, it got bitter. Nonetheless, she continued with this

God and found herself in Judah (Praise). Instead of giving room for bitterness, she praises her way through the tough times because she knows that when the going gets tough, the tough must get going since tough times never last—only tough people do. Eventually, God comes through for her, and she rises from the position of a beggar to the position of glory. In the same place she was following after reapers to glean for leftover grain, she marries and becomes the first lady of the Empire of Millionaire, Mr. Boaz.

CHAPTER 1

THE LAND OF MOAB

The land was ravaged by famine and a man from Bethlehem in Judah, together with his wife and two sons, relocated to the neighboring flourishing country of Moab.

Moabites, according to Jewish historians, belonged to the same stock as the Israelites. Their ancestral founder was Moab, a son of Lot, who was a nephew of the Israelite patriarch Abraham. However, they were idolaters; they worshipped a god named Chemosh, just as the Israelites worshipped Yahweh as their national God (Encyclopedia Britannica).

Elimelech and his wife, Naomi, and their two sons, Mahlon and Kilion, relocated to the alluring land of Moab without seeking God's face to know His will concerning the situation. They relocated, hoping for a better life for their family. Here we see a family faced with adversity and the decision made by the head of the family, supported by his wife. There was no mention of seeking God to know what to do, but instead they looked at the flourishing land of Moab next door and decided to relocate.

I have realized, however, that many times God allows us to go through difficulties for us to be mature in faith:

"….Count it all joy when you fall into various trials, knowing that the testing of your faith produces patience. But let patience have its perfect work, that you may be perfect and complete, lacking nothing." (James 1:2-4).

Many times, challenges are to strengthen our faith. God also promised us in Isaiah 43:2:

"When you pass through the waters, I will be with you;
And through the rivers, they shall not overflow you.
When you walk through the fire, you shall not be burned,
Nor shall the flame scorch you."

In Genesis 26:1-13, we see Isaac's different response to famine. The Lord appeared to him and instructed him not to go to Egypt, which must have been flourishing at that time, but to go to Gerar, a Philistine town situated on the border of Canaan. We were told that Isaac obeyed, remained, and sowed in the land, and that same year, he reaped a hundred-fold and was greatly blessed and favored by God. This is a result and the reward of obedience.

Often, when we go through difficult times, our response at those times is critical to our emergence from it at the end of the day. When Elimelech made this suggestion to relocate to Moab, Naomi, the wife, should have gone to God in prayer rather than just accepting her husband's decision. Sometimes women mistake submission to their husbands as just blindly following every decision. We should understand the fact that he is a man, and as such limited in every respect. Only God is all-seeing, all-knowing, and limitless. Therefore, it is important to take every decision to God in prayer and receive His leading.

This was one of the things that made King David successful in his walk with God and as a king. He always knew how to seek God for direction in difficult times, and God always gave Him victory as a result. Sometimes He allows us to go through adverse situations to toughen us up and teach us warfare as He did for the generation of Israelites who had not known war in Judges 3:1-3. This was His reason for leaving those nations in Canaan as a snare to Israel. However, God can help us navigate our way through difficult times and come out on the other side, better and richer if only we learn to trust Him. So, running away from the problem may not always be the solution; it is important to look to God for answers.

God can help us navigate our way through difficult times and come out on the other side, better and richer if only we learn to trust Him.

Unfortunately, Elimelech dies shortly after they got to the land of Moab, and Naomi is left with her two sons. She faces the challenge of being a single mother of two sons as well as being the breadwinner of the family. Life becomes tougher than when they were in Judah and she had her husband; the only difference is the availability of food.

A couple of years later, there is joy again in the home as Mahlon and Kilion get married. They married Moabite women; Orpah and Ruth. However, the joy is short-lived as the two sons die after about ten years of marriage without children. Naomi falls into depression and deep sorrow as a result.

Ruth, a promising young woman and a Moabitess, had met and married Mahlon, the son of Elimelech from Bethlehem, Judah. Like many young women her age, she had hoped to start having children after marriage. But instead of having children, she spent the first few years of marriage learning about the one true God, Jehovah, the God of Abraham, Isaac, and Jacob, whom her in-laws worshipped. Together with her husband, year after year, they believed that God would come through for them and bless them with children of their own, but it did not happen.

Year after year, her faith in God was growing, and she kept hoping against hope that each new year was 'the' year she would finally conceive. Each year it did not happen, but she did not give up. After their tenth wedding anniversary, suddenly her husband and brother-in-law died! What a devastating blow it must have been for her. *Lord, we believed and served you—where did we go wrong? Why Lord? Why did he have to die?* Many questions like this may have been going through her mind as she grieved her husband. *We trusted You for children and hoped to celebrate our tenth wedding anniversary with conception at least! Oh, Lord, why did he have to die?* Pain, disappointment, and sorrow of a young widow whose hopes had been dashed was her state.

Unfortunately, she had no child from their union, which would have been comforting at a time like this. It seemed like her world had come to an end.

Regrets

Naomi was feeling the worst hit of the three women because she had come to the Land of Moab with her husband and two sons with dreams, hopes, and aspirations of a better life with her family. But here she was, several years later, her husband dead and now her two sons as well! Was it a wrong move coming to Moab? Wasn't God in support of their relocation? Why did her husband and two sons die? *Oh, Lord, where do I go from here? Why am I still living? Oh Lord, this is too much for me!*

Our response during the time of adversity is important. God watches to see if we will seek Him for direction, or if we will solve the problem our own way. God wants to show His ability to keep us safe despite the difficulty. Unfortunately, many of us relocate without consulting God. We look for quick solutions that might end up giving us bigger problems in the long run, as we see in the case of Elimelech and Naomi. But God is merciful.

Naomi arises after mourning her two sons and decides to return to Judah with her daughters-in-law because she heard that the famine was over. However, as they set out, she tries to persuade her daughters-in-law to go back to their people because she had nothing more to offer them. After much persuasion, Orpah kisses her and said her goodbyes.

REFLECTIONS

1. Are there times you have made decisions without consulting God?

2. What were the consequences?

3. How would you approach the situation differently now?

4. What lessons have you learned from this chapter?

5. How will you apply lessons learned going forward?

NOTES

MY STORY:
THE BREAKING POINT

As a young woman living in England many years ago, I had been in an abusive relationship for about four years that produced two children. We were not married but living together because every time we planned for his parents to meet my family, his parents would refuse because I wasn't from their tribe and of course, they had their own candidate for him. My partner was in the habit of cheating on me. Whenever I confronted him about his cheating, we would get into an argument and he would get physically violent. When he calmed down, he would apologize for beating me and I would forgive him. This cheating continued, and at one point I began to lose confidence in myself, and I thought that perhaps I was not good enough for him. This led me to "hit the bottle."

Whenever he was away on one of those trips with another woman, I drank myself to sleep. After a while, I began to wish for death because I thought that there was nothing else to live for. Like Naomi, I was too blinded with the loss of the relationship that I failed to see my children and the need to live for their sakes. My cousin came over to my house after a while and spoke words that jolted me out of that state and made me stop taking my frustrations out on alcohol.

Like Naomi, I was too blinded with the loss of the relationship that I failed to see my children and the need to live for their sakes.

During one of his trips away, his other girlfriend, an African American, called from the United States after midnight (UK time) and wanted to speak to him. I simply told her that he wasn't in and dropped the phone. She called back and continued pestering me wanting to know if perhaps he had gone to another woman. I laughed and said yes to show her how it felt. Just then, I heard him open the door and let himself in. At that point, I told the woman on the line that he was back and that he had a lipstick stain on his shirt. (There wasn't a lipstick stain, but I wanted to make her feel how I had always felt when he was away with them.) On hearing that, he charged towards me and asked why I was lying, and he started hitting me.

In my pain, I grabbed his briefcase with his business documents because I knew how important that was to him. I opened it, and spilled water on the documents. That was a big mistake! He came at me, lifted me, and threw me on the floor. I was about six months pregnant at the time with our second child. I thought I would die. I thought I had died, actually! Our two-year-old daughter was crying and shouting all the while, "Daddy, stop hitting Mummy," and that cut my heart. I made up my mind that I did not want this life for my children. They deserve better. When he realized what he did, he picked me up and was apologetic, as always. However, that day my mind was made up to leave him and return home to Nigeria rather than remain in that relationship and end up being killed either by mistake or intentionally.

However, that day my mind was made up to leave him and return home to Nigeria rather than remain in that relationship and end up being killed either by mistake or intentionally.

Don't get me wrong, he was very kind, thoughtful, and generous. But unfortunately he just had this weakness when it came to women, and neither of us were committed Christians at that time. There was always an unexplainable spirit that came upon him whenever he started hitting me. When he finally came around, he would apologize and I would eventually forgive him.

After the birth of my son, unknown to him, I had started planning to leave him and return to Nigeria with my two children under the guise that we were going on holiday but I had no intention of coming back to him. I needed him to buy our tickets because I had no money, indeed no savings, since I had just been a student up to that point.

He was kind and generous and really provided a lot of comfort for the children and me. He paid for a nanny who lived on the outskirts of London to care for my daughter while I was going to college. But the relationship was heading nowhere with his parents' refusal to give their consent and insisting that he should first get married to their candidate before marrying me (I wasn't from their tribe, and that disqualified me). He kept refusing, though, and as a result they refused to give their consent for our marriage. This was our situation, and we had our two children in the process.

I had remained in the relationship because I thought that I had no other choice, especially with two children. But after that last beating when I was pregnant, I vowed never to give him that opportunity again. I told him I forgave him, but my heart was made up. It felt like any little feeling that I had left for him had been beaten off.

So I started making arrangements to return to Nigeria. He bought the tickets for me and the children thinking that we were just going to Nigeria on holiday, but I was resolute and there was no turning back. I needed to try another life. I could not continue for fear that I might die in the process. He gave us comfort, but comfort is not everything. I realized at this point that I would rather have less comfort and true love with a man who was not a womanizer. I was ready to face the tough times ahead with my children as we boarded the flight back to Nigeria.

I was resolute and there was no turning back. I needed to try another life.

CHAPTER 2

RETURN TO JUDAH

But Ruth said:
"Entreat me not to leave you,
Or to turn back from following after you;
For wherever you go, I will go;
And wherever you lodge, I will lodge;
Your people shall be my people,
And your God, my God."
(Ruth 1:16)

Often, it is not the failure or the falling that matters, but what you do afterward. The Bible says though the righteous fall seven times, he will always rise again (Proverbs 24:16). Failures, falls, disappointments, wrong decisions, and so forth, are all part of life and living. The important thing is that when we realize our wrong decisions and mistakes we must embark on the journey back to right our wrongs. Remaining there and murmuring, grumbling, and complaining will not solve anything, but rising from there and taking the needed steps back from where we fell is important.

Remaining there and murmuring, grumbling, and complaining will not solve anything, but rising from there and taking the needed steps back from where we fell is important.

Thus says the Lord:
"Stand in the ways and see,
And ask for the old paths, where the good way *is*,
And walk in it;
Then you will find rest for your souls.
But they said, 'We will not walk in it.'"
(Jeremiah 6:16)

Whenever we finally make up our mind to retrace our steps and make progress, it's important to note that doubts, fears, and negative thoughts will try to compel us to remain where we are or go back to the life we used to live, rather than have faith and trust in God as we return to Him. Naomi, in a moment of sorrow, was unknowingly trying to persuade her two daughters-in-law to go back to their "mother's home" which meant going back to the way of life they had always known and lived—a life of idol worship which the people of Moab practiced. Without knowing it, she was saying to them that the God they had come to know through their husbands had nothing to offer them. She thought that there was nothing left for them but hopelessness.

Orpah thought about it and figured that it was better to go back and at least marry from among her people, the Moabites, and continue the life she had always known before she became an Israelite by marriage. That was the last we ever heard of Orpah. When we figure out things with our limited understanding rather than trusting the unlimited God, we settle for less.

When we figure out things with our limited understanding rather than trusting the unlimited God, we settle for less.

Ruth, on the other hand, was of a different spirit. She was resolute, and her mind was made up about this God she had known. A great God who delivered His people from over 400 years of bondage in Egypt with great signs and wonders. A God who parted the Red Sea for the Israelites to walk on dry ground and caused the same water to overflow and drown the Egyptians, their Pharaoh, and his horsemen!

The Almighty God, the mighty man in battle who fights for his children and gives them victory over their enemies. She had heard about this God and believed everything about Him and yearned to follow Him to the end hence her response to her mother-in-law in Ruth 1:16:

> But Ruth said:
> "Entreat me not to leave you,
> Or to turn back from following after you;
> For wherever you go, I will go;
> And wherever you lodge, I will lodge;
> Your people *shall* be my people,
> And your God, my God."

The Bible says in Psalm 125:1:

> "Those who trust in the LORD
> Are like Mount Zion,
> Which cannot be moved, but abides forever."

Naomi stopped urging her to go back when she realized that Ruth was determined. That negative voice always fades away when it meets with determination.

Judah means praise, and Ruth chose to go the path of praise despite her sorrowful circumstance. When we decide to look away from our present circumstances and rather see the greatness of the God of possibilities, His power is provoked to work on our behalf.

When we decide to look away from our present circumstances and rather see the greatness of the God of possibilities, His power is provoked to work on our behalf.

"Let the peoples praise You, O God;
Let all the peoples praise You.
Then the earth shall yield her increase;
God, our own God, shall bless us.
God shall bless us,
And all the ends of the earth shall fear Him."
(Psalm 67:5-7)

So, they embarked on the journey back to Judah. They were sorrowful yet determined, not knowing what lay ahead of them, but at least they knew that the way they were going was the right way. Returning to Judah meant trusting God again and submitting their lives back to Him. Not remaining in the place of error or the place of sin is important. Being able to count your losses and retrace your steps is so vital to your progress and the future.

Being able to count your losses and retrace your steps is so vital to your progress and the future.

The Bible tells us in the book of Luke 15:11-32 about the story of the prodigal son who had asked his father to give him his portion of the inheritance. He took it and went away to a far country and squandered it all in riotous living. Then there was a famine in that land, and he had no more money. He got a job to feed and care for swine, and one day he was so hungry that he almost ate the food belonging to the swine, but the Bible said, "he came to his senses" and remembered that in his father's house, even the slaves had food to eat and so rather than die of hunger, he would make the journey back in repentance and ask his father for mercy. He then retraced his steps.

When we realize our errors, we must receive grace to humble ourselves, resist pride, and make the needed journey back in repentance.

When we realize our errors, we must receive grace to humble ourselves, resist pride, and make the needed journey back in repentance.

Naomi and Ruth both arrived in Bethlehem as the barley harvest was beginning.

Unconditional Love

In this story between Naomi and Ruth, we see God's agape love demonstrated. A love that loves the unlovable; a love that loves the poor and oppressed; the one no one wants to associate with. A love that knows no bounds; a love that goes all the way! Selfless love that never fails.

Such was the kind of love displayed by Ruth to her mother-in-law. People readily want to associate with the rich, famous, and successful ones. Most people avoid the ones in need, especially helpless widows like Naomi, who not only lost her husband but has also lost her two children in adulthood, leaving her empty and hopeless. But because God is ever merciful and gracious, a child of God is never completely down and out. God will always ensure that there is something that will help you rebound. Sometimes we need to look around and look closely—if you remain in Him, He will never leave you nor forsake you just as He promised in His word.

But because God is ever merciful and gracious, a child of God is never completely down and out

Help from Unusual Quarters

Ruth was that one "thing" that God left in Naomi's life, even though at that time, Naomi felt that she had nothing left. Like the widow of one of the sons of the prophets in 2 Kings 4:1-7 who cried out to Elisha that the creditors were coming to take her sons as slaves, Elisha asked her what she had, and she said, "Your maidservant has nothing in the house but a jar of oil."

Her first response was that she had nothing. She did not even consider the jar of oil as anything, and that was why she said "nothing, but a jar of oil." It was that same jar of oil that God used to turn around her situation.

She did not even consider the jar of oil as anything... It was that same jar of oil that God used to turn around her situation.

This is true for many of us. We look down on those things and those people that God has put around us to help us. Often God's packages come disguised, and it takes the spiritually discerning to see and recognize them. Naomi tried all she could to persuade both of her daughters-in-law to go back to their people and that she had nothing else to offer them. Orpah eventually yielded and went back, but Ruth saw this pitiful, bitter, helpless, poor woman and was committed to loving and caring for her regardless. In Ruth 1:21 Naomi said, "I went out full, and the LORD has brought me home again empty...." When we are going through challenges, we sometimes fail to see and acknowledge God's mercies despite it all.

Perhaps you are going through challenges right now, look around you and thank God for His mercies, even if they are just small mercies.

In-law Lessons

Ruth's love for her mother-in-law demonstrates the unconditional love that God expects between both groups of people, if they are genuinely born again and spirit-filled. You cannot look at the world and operate like the world does if you are a Spirit-filled child of God.

Mothers-in-law, if you truly walk in the fear of God, and love and serve God, then the spirit in you should be different. It should be a spirit of love, not that of judgment. The young lady is just starting a journey you began so many years ago. Imagine how it was for you when you just started—that is exactly how it is for her, if not worse because times have changed. The challenges of these times have increased. So rather than judge her, love and show her compassion. Ignore her errors. Pray for her—she needs your prayers if nothing else. Work towards a peaceful home for your son if you love him.

Likewise, daughters-in-law, do not enter the marriage with a worldly battle-ready mindset against your mother-in-law. It never pays off. God will not defend you, and you may just end up a casualty. I know of a young woman who followed that line of thinking, always fighting her mother-in-law and barring her from coming to their home, saying things like "leave my husband and me alone, please!" She eventually died under mysterious circumstances! Do not imagine that you can suddenly appear in the life of a young man and cut him off from the mother, father, siblings, or family that he has always known. If he were not cared for and educated, you would not desire him. Like I say to every young lady, you will also become a mother-in-law soon, so be careful the seeds you sow because you will reap a hundred-fold in the not-too-distant future.

Daughters-in-law, do not enter the marriage with a worldly battle-ready mindset against your mother-in-law... God will not defend you.

I once had a neighbor who had serious issues with her mother-in-law, who would insist on sitting in the front seat of the car if they were all going out and her husband was driving. Her mother-in-law also insisted on having a framed picture of herself in their living room. I agree that this is excessive on the part of the mother-in-law, but the solution is not in being confrontational with your mother-in-law, but in taking it all to God in prayer. This lady always confronted her mother-in-law. Finally, she got her husband to agree to relocate their family. She relocated to the United States with their children successfully, and her husband was to join them. However, a few days before his scheduled departure, he drove into the midst of a shootout between the police and armed robbers and got hit by a stray bullet. He died immediately and never joined his family. Rumor had it that her mother-in-law was responsible for his death. So, it was a case of "since I cannot see him again, you cannot have him either." These things really do happen.

The Bible says in 2 Cor. 10:4-5:

"For the weapons of our warfare are not carnal but mighty in God for pulling down strongholds, casting down arguments and every high thing that exalts itself against the knowledge of God…"

The Bible also says in Ephesians 6:12:

"For we do not wrestle against flesh and blood, but against principalities, against powers, against the rulers of the darkness of this age, against spiritual hosts of wickedness in the heavenly places."

When we have these scriptures at the back of our minds, then we will cease from fighting for ourselves and trust God for intervention by praying to God a lot more.

When we have these scriptures at the back of our minds, then we will cease from fighting for ourselves and trust God for intervention by praying to God a lot more.

I also remember a sister who was a member of a women's fellowship I have been coordinating for many years now. Whenever her mother-in-law was around, her husband would be with her in the guest room talking and catching up until he fell asleep! She would have to go wake him up to come up to their bedroom to sleep many times. Such was the closeness that he had with his mother, who also enjoyed showing this sister that the young man was first her son. But with prayers, God gave her wisdom to manage the relationship until the mother-in-law eventually passed on.

REFLECTIONS

1. Have you ever found yourself at a point where you know you need to retrace your steps, if so, what did you do?

2. How did you feel afterward?

3. During a difficult period, can you identify God's small mercies around you regardless?

4. Looking back, can you identify a disguised help that you almost missed or missed entirely?

5. If you are married, what is your relationship with your in-laws like?

6. How can you improve it, knowing that this is God's expectation from you?

NOTES

CHAPTER 3

TOUGH NEW BEGINNINGS

Ruth said to Naomi in Ruth 2:2, "Please let me go to the field, and glean heads of grain after him in whose sight I may find favor."

When they had both settled down in their new home, Ruth arose one morning and took permission from Naomi to go into the fields to glean after the harvesters so that she could return home with food. Naomi gave her blessings. Since both were widows, they needed to start taking care of themselves once again. Widows were considered the poorest in Israel in those days.

Ruth knew that since she was the younger one, she had to work to take care of both of them. This really speaks of a kind and selfless heart. She saw in Naomi a poor, helpless, and depressed woman, beaten and stripped of everything meaningful in her by life with nobody else in the world. So Ruth decided that she would take care of her and simply just take it one day at a time, trusting God for mercy.

Ruth knew that since she was the younger one, she had to work to take care of both of them. This really speaks of a kind and selfless heart.

Healing for the Broken-hearted

"The Spirit of the Lord God is upon Me,
Because the Lord has anointed Me
To preach good tidings to the poor;
He has sent Me to heal the brokenhearted,
To proclaim liberty to the captives,
And the opening of the prison to those who
are bound…"
(Isaiah 61:1)

There is nothing as painful to a woman than the loss of a husband, children, or both. Losing a husband is bad enough for Naomi, and just when she thought the worst was over, she experiences the loss of her two adult sons at the same time! No other blow could be more devastating than these. Therefore, she became embittered and slipped into depression.

Ruth, a young woman full of dreams and aspirations, also loses her husband after about ten years of marriage without a child. They were both trusting God with so much faith, and yet rather than conceive a child, her husband dies! Words cannot express the grief of this young woman. Her world suddenly turns around, and she must learn to live again, this time without her husband.

As these two women decided to return to Judah, they also decided to take their sorrow, their grief, and their pain to God. And as they cried their hearts out to Him every night with soaked pillows, He would envelop them with His arms of love, comforting and reassuring them that all will be well.

"Say to the righteous that it shall be well with them,
For they shall eat the fruit of their doings..."
(Isaiah 3:10).

And so, Ruth arms herself and finds strength in the word of God to go through each day.

REFLECTIONS

1. Have you ever found yourself in a situation that you needed to start all over again like Ruth and Naomi?

2. How did you feel, and What did you do?

3. How did you overcome temptations for more convenient choices?

4. How were you motivated to keep going when you felt like 'throwing in the towel'?

5. What lessons have you learned in this chapter?

6. How do you hope to apply it to your life?

NOTES

MY STORY: HE HEALS

I came back to Nigeria broken-hearted and deeply hurt. I felt betrayed by the one I had loved and trusted. I felt so much pain that I was not interested in any more relationships. I just wanted to work and take care of my two lovely God-given children.

Indeed, after we had arrived in Nigeria and I told him I was not coming back, he laughed at me in disbelief and asked who would marry me with two children. He said I was a joke and I had better come back with the children. That made me more determined to prove him wrong. I told him that if marriage was like what I had with him, I was not ever going to be interested. He told me that he was not going to give me money to support the children, and he would advise me to return.

He knew I had no savings and no help from anyone, so he tried using money to force me to return by refusing to care for the children if I did not return with them. Soon a friend invited me to her Pentecostal church—the Redeemed Christian Church of God, Apapa Parish at the time. When I got there it felt like coming home. This was what I had been looking for all my life. In all my troubles and confusion, I had been invited to other so-called "churches" like the Brotherhood of the Cross and Star in London, and I even tried to become a vegetarian like other members (even though I loved meat). After a few attempts, I realized that those were not for me, and I stopped attending. I had also tried the Celestial Church of Christ, which was very popular in the late eighties, but I also ran for my life when I saw some practices that were not in line with the teachings of the Bible—I knew that was not for me, either.

When I got there it felt like coming home. This was what I had been looking for all my life.

But when I entered this Pentecostal Church, I knew I was home. I saw like-minded beautiful young people like me who loved God with a passion. The message resonated with me, and when the altar call was made, I went out and submitted my life to the Lordship of Jesus Christ. Then I began to grow in Him, I began to hunger and thirst after His righteousness, and He filled me. Unlike previous experiences, I realized that serving God need not be burdensome. All the different requirements from the previous churches I had attended were not necessary. I did not need to go to the beach or stream to bathe to connect with God. I did not need to stop eating meat or have any special diet and most of all I could pray to God by myself and receive answers. I would study my Bible and pray regularly, and as a result I began to grow.

Unlike previous experiences, I realized that serving God need not be burdensome.

I also began to receive healing for my broken heart. I had hitherto shut the door to any relationships—I wasn't even interested in friendships—with men. But as I grew deep in my relationship with the Lord, He healed me and restored the desire for another go at marriage when the right time came. I was 22 years of age at that time.

CHAPTER 4

WHEN THE GOING GETS TOUGH, THE TOUGH GET GOING

The Lord then ordered Ruth's steps to the field belonging to Boaz, who was from the clan of Elimelech.

Ruth was obviously a hardworking young lady who was not afraid of tough choices. She could have decided to make other choices that may have been less stressful and more rewarding but offensive to her God. After all, she was a young lady. But she chose the path of hard work—going to the fields to glean after the reapers! She probably could have made more money as a prostitute, but that was not even an option for her because she loved God so much that offending Him was the last thing she wanted. When our heart is right and trusting God, He gives us the grace to do the right things even when it is not convenient.

When our heart is right and trusting God, He gives us the grace to do the right things even when it is not convenient.

In no time, her reputation as a hard worker became known, and she made a good impression on the harvesters. When Boaz arrived in his field, he noticed her and inquired after her from his harvesters. His manager gave him a good report about how hardworking she had been, and further told him about how she had shown kindness to her mother-in-law, Naomi, in leaving her people and the land of her birth to return with her to take care of her.

By now, Boaz was really impressed with all he had heard, and said to Ruth, "You will listen, my daughter, will you not? Do not go to glean in another field, nor go from here, but stay close by my young women. Let your eyes be on the field which they reap, and go after them. Have I not commanded the young men not to touch you? And when you are thirsty, go to the vessels and drink from what the young men have drawn." (Ruth 2:8-9). On seeing and hearing all about her, he felt protective over her and looked upon her with favor. He observed her calm and humble demeanor and knew she was different. He instructed his men not to touch her and advised her to stay close to his servant girls.

Sometimes we are just busy doing what is right, and we do not know that people are watching and taking note, and most of all, God is taking note. As Christians, God expects us to care for the poor and needy.

Sometimes we are just busy doing what is right, and we do not know that people are watching and taking note, and most of all, God is taking note.

"He who has pity on the poor lends to the Lord,
And He will pay back what he has given."
(Proverbs 19:17)

"But do not forget to do good and to share, for with such sacrifices God is well pleased." (Hebrews 13:16)

One of the most common ways of identifying a true Christian is one with a heart of love and genuine compassion. One who is selfless and genuinely cares for the good of others. Such was the heart of Ruth. It is indeed never popular and convenient to care for a poor widow who had no one else.

One of the most common ways of identifying a true Christian is one with a heart of love and genuine compassion... Such was the heart of Ruth.

Ruth had many other options that she could have taken but she chose the option of showing selfless love and compassion to someone else even though she was also grieving at the time. She knew that her own situation was still better than Naomi's because she was younger and still had hopes of remarrying someday. Naomi was old with no husband or child to care for her. Such was her pitiful state, but Ruth decided to care for her as her own mother.

"Now Boaz said to her at mealtime, 'Come here, and eat of the bread, and dip your piece of bread in the vinegar.' So she sat beside the reapers, and he passed parched grain to her; and she ate and was satisfied, and kept some back."

(Ruth 2:14). Unknown to Ruth, things have already started happening fast in the spirit realm. It is most unusual to pay so much attention to a stranger who would have been considered even beneath his servants. A man of Boaz's standing would, under normal circumstances, not bat an eyelid over a Moabitess who strayed into his field. But God had orchestrated the meeting. Without knowing it, something had begun in the spirit realm, and that was why he went above and beyond to ensure her comfort and safety. He went a step further and invited her to their table for a meal.

In Israel, in those days, the widows were the poorest. She must have been looking really poor and wretched. Mr. Boaz, on the other hand, was in a position to get any woman of his choice, but he noticed and saw something different in this young Moabitess widow who had strayed into his field for food! He also ordered his men to make an allowance for her to take some actual stalks from the bundles. She gathered so much barley that when she got home, Naomi could not help asking where she had gleaned that day to have gathered so much. Ruth told her that the man's name is Boaz.

"The Lord bless him!" Naomi said to her daughter-in-law. She told Ruth that Boaz is a close relative, and a kinsman-redeemer. She advised her to remain in his field until the end of the wheat and barley harvest, just as Boaz had instructed her.

REFLECTIONS

1. What has kept you on the straight and narrow path?

2. Can you list things you can get motivation from during difficult times?

3. Can you list the qualities Ruth had that made her stand out? Remember, she was not looking stunning in terms of outward appearance, but she had some other inner beauty. Identify them and prayerfully ask God for help in those areas.

4. What lessons have you learned in this chapter?

5. How do you intend to apply it to your life?

NOTES

MY STORY: TOUGH CHOICES

Starting all over with two children was tough, but I was determined to see it through and not go back or opt for convenient options that would offend God. I stayed briefly with a friend and her family. After a few months I moved into a room in an apartment that a family friend rented for his aged mother who needed daily assistance from some maids. This place was located on the back side of Lagos, an area I never realized existed. I believe God needed to bring me down to this point to humble me thoroughly in order to make me a better person for the assignment ahead.

 Even though I had lost my father at an early age of seven compared with my two sisters, I still had a good life with my older half-sister and her family. She was my father's first child and like a mother to me. I went to one of the best high schools at that time (owned and operated by the federal government of Nigeria—a Federal Government Girls' College). But I had to leave after my high school graduation to try to figure out the rest of my life by myself. It was at this point that I met the father of my children who was living in London and made arrangements for me to join him there. He offered to sponsor my post-secondary education, and I was admitted into Kensington College of Business in South West London. Growing up in Nigeria, I only knew the inner-city areas of Lagos because my sister and her family lived on Bode Thomas in the 70's and moved to the 5th Avenue area of Festac Town in the early 80's, which was one of the best gated communities in Lagos in those days. In London, we lived on Edgware Road, very close to Oxford Street, West London, which was the posh side of London.

But here I was in the middle of a semi-slum area with my children. It was tough coming to terms with living here. Every attempt to get a loan to rent a better accommodation proved futile, and I kept feeling frustrated until one day God spoke to me through a friend. She said God said that I should stop fighting where I was but settle down there for now and make the most of it. She advised me to fix up the room, change the curtains, put in a TV for the children, and make it comfortable for us since the rest of the house always smelled because of the old lady's incontinence. So I received deliverance and entered God's rest about my accommodation. However, I was never quick to invite anyone to my place, and whoever dared to ask at church, I would nicely dance around it.

I got a job and enrolled the children in school. My life simply revolved around work, church, and home. I cut off all forms of social activities and friends who were not interested in being born again. I knew only God could help me, and I needed to focus on Him, live right, and develop myself spiritually. The choices I made were tough, but by this time, I knew the world had nothing to offer but vanity upon vanity, and I had had enough of it all. Gradually I became a volunteer at church.

I knew only God could help me, and I needed to focus on Him, live right, and develop myself spiritually.

At some point, I was in between jobs and started a business. Initially, business was good—I was supplying corporate gifts to companies. I remember waking up one day and all I had was less than 500 Nigerian Naira (less than $2 US), and I cried out to God. I needed to give my maid money to pick the children up from school by taxi. (As for myself, I usually commuted by bus, but since the children had always known comfort, I would always send them to and from school in a taxi.) By the time I deducted about 200 or 300 Naira for a taxi for the day for the children, I did not have much left, and we still needed to cook! And so, as usual, I woke up early that morning and had my devotion crying out to God in prayer for mercy and provision. I reminded Him that He promised to take care of the children and me as our Jehovah Jireh (the Lord our provider). I had made a covenant with God that I would not enter into any relationship that would mean depending on any man for money, and so He would prove Himself to me by being our Provider, taking care of our needs.

I stepped out with a sample of a leather bag that some-one had ordered for herself with intentions of paying at the end of the month. So I decided to visit a friend in her office that morning before going on to deliver the bag to the person who ordered it. As I was speaking with my friend, a colleague of hers came into her office, saw the leather bag I was hold-ing, and asked if it was for sale. My first reaction was to say no because I was taking it to the lady who had ordered it, but the Holy Spirit reminded me that I said I needed money, and I could get more of these bags from the supplier. I promptly said yes it was for sale. She asked about the price and I told her 3000 Naira. She was excited and took the one I was hold-ing and paid me cash for it and also ordered an additional one for her friend and gave me a check for that. I could not believe such an immediate answer to my prayer. That was two bags sold for 6000 Naira, and I would still get another one for the lady who had initially ordered with intentions of paying at the end of the month. This was one of my first experiences of God as our provider. Hallelujah!

This was one of my first experiences of God as our provider. Hallelujah!

Indeed, this was a period of wilderness for me, and I experienced God in different ways. This was one of my best seasons with the Lord because He manifested Himself to me as my Provider, my Healer, my Peace. Psalm 23 says, "The Lord is my Shepherd; I shall not want…."

Naturally, I had several male advances but I had decided I was not going to enter into any relationship without God anymore. If I had a choice, I just wanted to take care of my children with Jesus as my everything. Once beaten twice shy, as they say. Besides, I did not want to be like the Samaritan woman in John 4:1–18 who met Jesus by the well, and when asked to call her husband, she said that she had no husband. Jesus confirmed that to be true and indeed said she had been through five marriages, and the current one is still not hers! That is exactly what happens when we keep trying to find love in our strength and with our limited knowledge.

CHAPTER 5

DIVINE CONNECTIONS

"... My daughter, shall I not seek security for you.... Therefore wash yourself and anoint yourself, put on your best garment and go down to the threshing floor... " (Ruth 3:1-3)

This was timeless advice from an older woman to a much younger one. Today, such opportunities are rare because most youths believe that they know everything about relationships, dating, and courtship and do not need advice from their mothers, guardians, or spiritual leaders and mentors.

Ruth had shown kindness to Naomi, and payback time had come. Sometimes God rewards us through the same person we have shown kindness to, but many times not necessarily. Whatever the case, it is important to know that there is always payback time. The Bible says, "... whatever a man sows, that he will also reap." (Galatians 6:7). If you sow kindness and love, you will reap the same, and if evil, you will also reap the same. Ruth had selflessly cared for Naomi, and then one day Naomi arose and decided to give the motherly instructions that will lead her into her own home.

If you sow kindness and love, you will reap the same, and if evil, you will also reap the same.

Apart from being a kindhearted, loving, and generous woman, Ruth was also very humble and obedient. God had dealt with her so much that she had become thoroughly humbled by the things she had suffered. God had brought her down from the place of a beautiful woman with a dream of having children of her own for her prince charming to one who just wanted to do the will of God. She simply walked in humility and love and cared for her helpless old mother-in-law. She was not sure of anything anymore but that she loved God and only wanted to please Him and do His will. Her life was yielded to the promptings of the Holy Spirit.

Many young ladies do not yield to the promptings of the Holy Spirit because their flesh is still in control of their lives. They still want to choose who to marry by themselves. If all the boxes do not check out, they reject and resist God's will for them, because their judgment is based on material things and physical appearances. "...For the Lord does not see as man sees; for man looks at the outward appearance, but the Lord looks at the heart." (1 Samuel 16:7). He alone knows who will make a good and godly wife or husband. He knows who will live long and who will die the very next day. Only God knows because he is the Omniscience God (All-Knowing God). As His children, we need to be more yielded to His leadings and trust His instructions to us.

The threshing floor was a flat smooth and hard surface where, after harvest, the grain was separated from the straw and husks by beating it manually because there was no machinery in those biblical days. So Naomi got wind of the fact that Boaz will be on the threshing floor to supervise his men on that day and felt it was a good opportunity for Ruth to meet him there. She instructed her to take her bath, to wear her best clothes, and to put on some nice perfume.

Sometimes some women downplay the need to look and smell nice and hence do not take care of themselves. Some go about with a body odor that repulses whoever comes near them. A woman is likened to a flower, and just as flowers look beautiful and smell nice, a woman must always look and smell like a flower. Some Christian sisters take a lot of things for granted, even after marriage. Have you ever wondered why a strange woman would take your husband away from you? Strange women spend quality-time caring for their bodies, and whenever they step out, it is in style and smelling nice, too. Naomi may be old, but she was once young. She had been through this stage of life that Ruth was in and was in the best position to advise her on what to do.

Boaz was obviously much older than Ruth and would probably have never made the first move for fear of being refused or called a cradle snatcher. Some would argue that Ruth's move was improper, and I would like to correct this. Sometimes men need to see that the feeling is mutual, especially in a case like this where the man is much older. She was also acting on instruction from Naomi, who was like her mother and guardian and an older woman in the faith. So this may also have been the Holy Spirit initiating the move towards Boaz. Here she was now looking and smelling nicer than when they had first met.

Boaz also, without doubt, had been thinking of her since their first meeting and did not resist her, but immediately responded favorably. He even sent her back to her mother-in-law with a huge gift.

As Christians, humility is a major determinant of how far we would go with the help of God.

Ruth's humble disposition made it possible for her to be advised by Naomi. This was what also made it possible for her to act in obedience. As Christians, humility is a major determinant of how far we would go with the help of God. Therefore, it is always important to remain humble and relate with people in humility. It has everything to do with our achieving God's desired goals for us. The Bible says:

"...God resists the proud,
But gives grace to the humble."
(1 Peter 5:5)

REFLECTIONS

1. Do you commune with the Holy Spirit?

2. How can you identify His leadings?

3. Have there been times the Holy Spirit told you to do something, and you felt it was ridiculous?

4. Did you obey all the same and what was the outcome?

5. What lessons have you learned in this chapter?

6. How do you hope to apply it to your life?

NOTES

MY STORY: DIVINE ARRANGEMENTS

I remember visiting a sister, a member of my church, at her workplace (an oil company—I was looking for a business opportunity) one beautiful sunny day, and as we were in the parking lot about to leave, she looked towards her colleague behind us who was about to enter his own vehicle. She asked me if I knew that brother behind us, that he was a brother in church and a widower. I looked at him but he did not look familiar. I noticed how the trousers he had on did not fit correctly, and I told my friend that I did not know him, but he sure needs a wife. We smiled and drove off. Dressing up has always been a passion for me, and I would readily notice anything that escaped the scrutiny of other people. The outfit was not bad, just that he had outgrown it as far as I was concerned.

A few weeks later, I spoke with someone in church about investing in the company I was working in, and he referred me to Bro Femi, who was standing as an usher in church. So I walked up to bro Femi just before he left church and asked for an appointment to see him in his office and that I had a business proposition for him. He obliged me.

On that fateful day, I woke up early as usual and had my devotion. I committed the meeting before God and trusted Him that I hoped to finally get an investor for the company that I was working with. I got to his office on time, and as we were talking he smiled apologetically and told me he was in the middle of a project (building his house), and every penny he had was going into it. He saw how disappointed I looked and quickly added that he would bear it in mind when he was ready for investments again.

Well, that lightened the mood, and we then started discussing other things and realized that we were both single parents. We talked about how we were trying to cope and how interesting our children were. This was how our friendship started. We exchanged numbers and he would call me often for a chat, and of course we would exchange greetings in church. It was much later that I realized he was the same guy that my friend and I had seen in their company parking lot the day I had visited her. I saw him from a distance, and it was his trousers that stuck out to me on that day.

I left the investment company I was working with and got another job in another company, and this time the job came with an almost brand-new company car and a driver as well as some other perks. I had been praying for a car but did not realize how God was going to answer me.

A friend and a sister in church, Nneka (of blessed memory now) whose husband owned a vehicle sales and marketing company, had been trying to persuade me to come and work at their company, but I resisted, wanting something else. Eventually I began to feel unfulfilled in my investment job, and I knew it was time to leave. I called Nneka and asked what the package they were offering looked like, and as soon as she told me, I knew this could only be by God! A car at last and a very good one at that, an almost-brand-new Racer Daewoo. I had been back in Nigeria and actively in church for two years by then, and God had kept showing me His love and mercies.

I had been back in Nigeria and actively in church for two years by then, and God had kept showing me His love and mercies.

CHAPTER 6

A GLORIOUS DESTINATION

"... You are witnesses this day." (Ruth 4:10)

At the time of their return to Judah, Naomi felt bitter because she had gone to the land of Moab with her husband and two sons but was returning several years later empty, with her husband and two sons dead. Feeling bitter and empty and not even appreciating the fact that at least she had her daughter-in-law Ruth with her. They entered Judah at harvest time, but it was a time of barrenness in their personal lives.

Judah means "Praise." Despite their adversity, they repositioned themselves to the place of praise. Psalm 67:5-7 tells us that as we praise God, He causes the earth to yield its increase to us. This is exactly what began to happen in the life of Ruth and Naomi. The Lord now begins to orchestrate things to give their lives a brand-new beginning.

Judah means "Praise." Despite their adversity, they repositioned themselves to the place of praise.

God always turns our setbacks to comebacks. The point at which you lose hope and think there is nothing left is the exact point God begins to do glorious work to turn the tide in your favor. If you continue in Him, He is merciful and faithful. He is the one who is able to make a way where there seems to be no way. The Israelites thought that they had hit a dead end with the Pharaoh and the Egyptians pursuing hard behind them and the Red Sea before them. They thought all hope was lost, and they will all soon be dead men. But because God is the Almighty who is the Omnipotent (has divine abilities) and the only wise God. He made a way through the sea for the Israelites to work through dry land and caused the same sea to drown the Pharaoh, his horsemen, and chariots. What a Mighty God we serve. That God is still on the Throne and still doing wonders in the life of

His children who dare to take a stand for Him and not compromise their faith.

God always turns our setbacks to comebacks. The point at which you lose hope and think there is nothing left is the exact point God begins to do glorious work to turn the tide in your favor.

Boaz sets in motion everything to fulfill all righteousness and then marries Ruth.

Ruth 4:13 tells us that after she became his wife, he went in to her and the Lord enabled her to conceive! This is the same person that had tried conceiving for over ten years during her first marriage.

God indeed is the Master Planner of our lives. He knows the very end from the very beginning.

"For I know the thoughts that I think toward you, says the LORD, thoughts of peace and not of evil, to give you a future and a hope." (Jeremiah 29:11).

When we are going through difficult and trying times, sometimes we may not know the reason. But as we keep walking with God, loving and obeying Him, eventually things begin to make sense and He causes all things to work together for our good (Romans 8:28).

I have since realized that huge testimonies take longer to cook! We only need to be patient with God. Ruth gave birth to a son, and Naomi's world turns around for good. She took him, nursed, and cared for the child. The same women who could not recognize her when she returned to Judah were there to rejoice with her. "…'There is a son born to Naomi.' And they called his name Obed. He is the father of Jesse, the father of David." (Ruth 4:17). This was the beginning of the lineage through which Jesus Christ would come.

Ruth, a foreigner from Moab, becomes the great grand-mother of David, Israel's most celebrated king.

Ruth, a foreigner from Moab, becomes the great grandmother of David, Israel's most celebrated king.

REFLECTIONS

1. Have you ever been at the edge of a breakthrough and given up ?

2. What happened?

3. What lessons have you learned in this chapter?

4. How do you hope to apply it to your daily life?

NOTES

MY STORY: A YIELDED LIFE

"... My counsel shall stand..."
(Isaiah 46:10)

Indeed, God is great and to be greatly feared. The scripture above, in a nutshell, says that it is His plans that would eventually come to pass over our lives. So, what a wise Christian does is to find out His will and simply live a yielded life in humility and obedience to His leadings.

Femi and I had been friends for a few months, spending long hours just chatting and sometimes going to Ghana High Commission for lunch (there was a popular food joint behind the old Ghana High Commission in Lagos). Suddenly I began to look forward to his calls. When on a particular day I had not heard from him, I called him. When he picked the phone, I felt foolish and did not know what to say. I quickly mumbled, "Hi, just checking up on you," and I dropped the call, sweating profusely because I had been taught that it is the guy that calls, not the lady.

With hindsight now, though, honestly, when you have established a friendship, it should not matter who calls first anymore. I later discovered that he had not called because he was also beginning to feel the same way about me as I was feeling about him, and had started praying fervently for God to take away the feeling if the relationship was not of God. Incidentally, I was also praying the same prayers privately. I remember going to one of the monthly Holy Ghost Services at the RCCG Redemption Camp along the Lagos—Ibadan express road, a gathering of hundreds of thousands of people—and I said to God that if he is your choice for me, let me see him in this crowd. I had barely finished praying that prayer as we were heading for the auditorium. I saw him coming like he had seen me and was heading my way. I almost fainted because this was a place where hundreds of people gather monthly for a Night Virgil. If God did not divinely position him, there is no way we would have met at such a gathering. By now, I knew that I needed to intensify my prayers, which is basically for God to stop everything that is not of Him.

If God did not divinely position him, there is no way we would have met at such a gathering.

Five months after our friendship started, he proposed to me. That was in November, and by January the following year we were married. Our bridal train were his three children and my two. Some years later we had two additional children and by God's grace they are seven in total: God's number of perfection.

By the time we got married he had just moved into our newly built home, fully furnished by the company he was working with at that time. For some reason my room was the best in the house! So God finally moved me from that accommodation I detested to our newly-built home with my room complete and awaiting my arrival. What a Mighty God we serve!

TOUGH TIMES NEVER LAST, BUT TOUGH PEOPLE DO!

"For whatever things were written before were written for our learning, that we through the patience and comfort of the Scriptures might have hope." (Romans 15:4)

The book of Ruth in the Holy Bible was put there so that you and I can find hope and strength in times of hopelessness. Sometimes the death of a loved one can seem like our world has come to an end, and there is nothing more to live for. But God is able to launch us into a wonderful new beginning.

God's ways are not our ways, and if we continue in Him, He can give us beauty for ashes, the oil of joy for mourning, a garment of praise for the spirit of heaviness (Isaiah 61:3).

At that point, where it seems like the world has come to an end for you, God is able to step into your life and give you a brand new beginning if only you believe.

Where it seems like the world has come to an end for you, God is able to step into your life and give you a brand new beginning if only you believe.

Perhaps you want to start by inviting Jesus into your life. Please pray after me:

Lord Jesus, please forgive all my sins. Wash me with your blood and please come into my life afresh. From this day onwards I want to live for you. I surrender my life to you Lord. Thank you, Lord, in Jesus' name. Amen.

If you prayed that prayer, huge congratulations to you! Your life is about to change for the better as Jesus steps in and takes over. But mind you it is not going to be easy all the way but His grace will see you through. Buy a complete Bible with old and new Testament and start reading. Know that you can go to God in prayers through Jesus Christ. Also ask the Lord to lead you to a Bible believing church around you. There are many Spirit filled messages on YouTube you can also access by great men and women of God like Pastor E. A. Adeboye, Bishop David Oyedepo, Bishop T.D. Jakes, Joel Osteen, and Joyce Meyers, to mention a few.

RESOURCES

For speaking engagements and to share your testimonies with me, I can be reached at **info@elsieotegbade.com**.

For more information, please visit my website:

www.elsieotegbade.com

YOU ARE VICTORIOUS!